WEALTH WISE;
A STEP BY STEP GUIDE TO
ACHIEVING FINANCIAL FREEDOM

TAY LOR

All rights reserved. No part of this publication may be reproduced, distributed, or transmitted in any form or by any means, including photocopying, recording, or other electronic or mechanical methods, without the prior written permission of the publisher, except in the case of brief quotations embodied in critical reviews and certain other noncommercial uses permitted by copyright law.

Copyright © (Tay Lor), (2024)

TABLE OF CONTENTS

CHAPTER 1

CHAPTER 2

CHAPTER 3

CHAPTER 4

CHAPTER 5

CHAPTER 6

CHAPTER 7

CHAPTER 8

INTRODUCTION

Welcome to " Wealth Wise: A Step-by-Step Guide to Achieving Financial Freedom"!

Are you uninterested in living paycheck to paycheck? Do you dream of economic protection and freedom? You're now no longer alone. Many people conflict with coping with our budget, saving fordestiny, and constructing wealth. But it would not have to be that way.

In This book, We're going to tell you that accomplishing economic freedom is inside your reach. You'll find out how to:

- Create a financial that works for you, now no longer in opposition to you

- Invest for your destiny and construct wealth

- Save for retirement and obtain economic protection

- Manage debt and credit score like a pro

- Start a facet hustle or commercial enterprise to enhance your income

- Develop a wealth attitude and conduct to obtain long- time period success

Our intention is to empower you with the knowledge, tools, and self assurance to take manageyour budget and construct a wealthy destiny. Whether you are simply beginning out or nearing retirement, this ee-e book is your roadmap to economic freedom.

So, let's getout on this adventure together!

CHAPTER 1

SETTING FINANCIAL GOALS

" Setting desires is step one in turning the invisible into the visible. " - Tony Robbins

Financial desires are used to achieve monetary freedom. Without clean desires, you are like a delivery with out a rudder, drifting aimlessly. In this chapter, we will discover the significance of placing monetary desires and manual you via a step- through-step method to set your own.

Why Set Financial Goals?

- Clarity and direction

- Motivation and focus

- Measurable progress

- Increased confidence

- Achieving monetary freedom

Identifying Your Values and Priorities

- What topics maximum to you in life?

- What type of life-style do you need to lead?

- What are your non-negotiable?

Creating a Vision for Your Financial Future

- Imagine your best monetary life

- What does its appearance look like?

- How does it feel?

Setting SMART Goals

- Specific

- Measurable

- Achievable

- Relevant

- Time-bound

Examples of SMART Goals:

- Save $10,000 for a down price on a residence in the subsequent 12 months

- Pay off credit score card debt of $five,000 in the subsequent 6 months

- Increase earnings by 20% in the subsequent 12 months

Take Action!

- Write down your values and priorities

- Describe your imagination and prescient in your monetary future

- Set 3- five SMART desires

By placing clean monetary desires, you may be focused, motivated, and empowered to obtain monetary freedom. In the following chapter, we will discover budgeting and cost management, the vital gear for reaching your monetary desires.

CHAPTER 2

BUDGETING AND EXPENSE MANAGEMENT

" Finance isn't always a restriction, but a liberation. " - Unknown

Budgeting and rate control are the spine of attaining economic freedom. In this chapter, we will discover the significance of budgeting, a way to create a budget that works for you, and powerful rate control. strategies.

The 50/30/20 Rule

- 50% for essential fees (housing, utilities, food)

- 30% for discretionary spending (entertainment, hobbies)

- 20% for saving and debt repayment

Creating a Budget That Works for You

- Identify your profits and fees

- Categorize fees into wishes and wants

- Set economic desires and priorities

- Assign greenback quantities to every category

- Regularly evaluation and adjust

Expense Management Strategies

- Track your fees

- Prioritize wishes over wants

- Cut useless fees

- Use the envelope system

- Avoid impulse purchases

Common Budgeting Mistakes

- Not accounting for abnormal fees

- Underestimating fees

- Not prioritizing wishes over wants

- Not often reviewing and adjusting

Take Action!

- Write down your profits and fees

- Create a finance the usage of the 50/30/20 rule

- Identify regions for rate reduction

- Implement rate control strategies

By developingfinances and handling fees effectively, you may be on top of things in your budget and on course to achieve your economic desires. In the following chapter, we will discover makinginvestment and wealth creation, the important thing to constructing long- time period economic security.

CHAPTER 3

INVESTING AND WEALTH CREATION

" Investing is the important thing to unlocking economic freedom. " - Unknown

Investing and wealth introduction are essential steps in reaching economic freedom. In this chapter, we will discover the sector of making an investment, exceptional funding options, and techniques for constructing wealth.

Understanding Investing

- Investing vs. saving

- Risk and return

- Diversification

Investment Options

- Stocks

- Bonds

- Real property

- Mutual funds

- Exchange-traded funds (ETFs)

- Retirement accounts (401(k), IRA)

Strategies for Building Wealth

- Start early

- Be consistent

- Diversify your portfolio

- Educate your self

- Avoid get-rich- short schemes

Investing for Beginners

 - Start withstable information for making an investment

- Begin with a small amount

- Consider a robo-advisor

- Keep fees low

Advanced Investing Strategies

- Dollar- price averaging

- Value Making an investment

- Dividend making an investment

- Real property making an investment

Take Action!

- Open a brokerage account

- Start making an investment with a small amount

- Educate yourself on making an investment

- Diversify your portfolio

- Avoid getting stuck up in get-rich- short schemes

By making an investment and constructing wealth , you may be growing a stable economic destiny and reaching economic freedom. In the following chapter, we will discover saving and retirement planning, crucial steps in securing your economic destiny.

CHAPTER 4

SAVING AND RETIREMENT PLANNING

" Saving is the most important thing to monetary freedom. " - Unknown

Saving and retirement Making plans is an important step in accomplishing monetary freedom. In this chapter, we're going to discover the significance of saving, distinct financial savings options, and techniques for retirementplans.

Understanding Saving

- Emergency fund

- Short- time period financial savings

- Long- time period financial savings

- Retirement Financial savings

Savings Options

- High-yield financial savings accounts

- Certificates of deposit (CDs)

- Money marketplace accounts

- Individual retirement accounts (IRAs)

- 401(k) and different corporation- backed plans

Retirement Planning Strategies

- Start early

- Take benefit of corporation matching

- Consider a Roth IRA

- Invest in a varied portfolio

- Review and modify your plan frequently

Retirement Planning Mistakes to Avoid

- Not beginning early enough

- Not taking benefit of corporation matching

- Not diversifying your portfolio

- Not frequently reviewing and adjusting your plan

Take Action!

- Open a high-yield financial savings account

- Start a retirement account

- Take benefit of corporation matching

- Invest in a varied portfolio

- Review and modify your plan frequently

By saving and making plans for retirement, you will be developing a stable monetary destiny and accomplishing monetary freedom. In the subsequent chapter, we're going to discover dealing with debt and credit, vital steps in retaining monetary stability.

CHAPTER 5

MANAGING DEBT AND CREDIT

" Managing debt and credit scores is essential for economic stability. " - Unknown

Managing debt and credit score is an important thing to accomplishing economic freedom. In this chapter, we're going to discover techniques for handling debt, know-how credit score reports, and constructing a sturdy creditscore.

Understanding Debt

- Types of debt (credit score, playing cards, loans, mortgages)

- Debt snowball method

- Debt avalanche method

- Consolidating debt

Understanding Credit

- Credit reports

- Credit scores

- Factors affecting credit score scores

- Credit usage ratio

Building a Strong Credit Score

- Make on-time payments

- Keep credit score usage low

- Monitor credit score reports

- Avoid useless inquiries

- Build a credit score mix

Managing Credit Cards

- Avoid overspending

- Pay off balances in full

- Use rewards wisely

- Avoid annual fees

- Considerstability transfer

Take Action!

- Create a debt reimbursement plan

- Check your credit score report

- Dispute Any errors

- Make a plan to construct your credit score

- Use credit score playing cards responsibly

By handling debt and credit score effectively, you will be taking a sizable step in the direction of accomplishing economic freedom. In the subsequent chapter, we're going to discover the significance of coverage and danger control in securing your economic future.

CHAPTER 6

INSURANCE AND RISK MANAGEMENT

" Insurance is the protection of your economic destiny. " - Unknown

Insurance and chance control are vital additives to accomplishing economic freedom. In this chapter, we will discover the distinct forms of coverage, a way to verify chance, and techniques for handling chance.

Types of Insurance

- Life coverage

- Health coverage

- Disability coverage

- Homeowners coverage

- Auto coverage

Assessing Risk

- Identify capability risks

- Evaluate the chance of chance

- Determine the capability effect of chance

- Develop a chance control plan

Strategies for Managing Risk

- Diversification

- Hedging

- Insurance

- Asset allocation

- Regular evaluate and adjustment

Life Insurance

- Term lifestyle coverage

- Whole lifestyle coverage

- Universal lifestyle coverage

- Variable lifestyles coverage

Health Insurance

- Individual fitness coverage

- Group fitness coverage

- Medicare

- Medicaid

Take Action!

- Assess your chance control needs

- Research and examine coverage options

- Consult with an economic advisor

- Implement a chance control plan

- Regularly evaluate and regulate your plan

By handling chance and securing good enoughcoverage, you will be shielding your economic destiny and accomplishing peace of mind. In the subsequent chapter, we will discover the significance of property making plans and legacy building.

CHAPTER 7

ESTATE PLANNING AND LEGACY BUILDING

" Your legacy isn't pretty much what you go away behind, no matter the way you live your life. " - Unknown

Estate making plans and legacy construction are vital factors in accomplishing economic freedom. In this chapter, we're going to discover the significance of property making plans, wills, trusts, and legacy constructing strategies.

Importance of Estate Planning

- Protecting your assets

- Ensuring your desires are achieved

- Minimizing taxes and fees

- Providing for cherished ones

Wills and Trusts

- Last will and testament

- Revocable residing trust

- Irrevocable trust

- Living will

Legacy Building Strategies

- Creating a legacy statement

- Building a basis or charity

- Establishing a scholarship or award

- Writing a letter or video for cherished ones

Additional Estate Planning Considerations

- Powers of attorney

- Beneficiary designations

- Funeral making plans

- Digital asset management

Take Action!

- Consult with a property making plan attorney

- Create a will and trust

- Establish a legacy constructing strategy

- Review and replace your property plan regularly

- Consider developing a legacy letter or video

By making plans for your property and constructing a legacy You will be making sure that your desires are achieved and have an enduring effect on your family and community. In the very last chapter, we're going to discover the significance of givingand creating an effective effect on the world.

CHAPTER 8

GIVING BACK AND MAKING A POSITIVE IMPACT

" The great way to locate yourself is to loseself inside the carrier of others. " - Mahatma Gandhi

Giving again and creating an effective effect on the arena is a satisfying way to acquire economic freedom. In this bankruptcy, we're going to discover the significance of giving, one of a kind approaches to offer again, and the blessings of philanthropy.

Importance of Giving

- Helping others in need

- Making an effective effect on your community

- Leaving a long-lasting legacy

- Personal boom and fulfillment

Ways to Give Back

- Volunteering your time

- Donating to charity

- Mentoring or coaching

- Community carrier

Benefits of Philanthropy

- Tax blessings

- Personal fulfillment

- Networking opportunities

- Legacy building

Strategies for Effective Giving

   - Research and perceive respectable charities

- Set clean dreams and objectives

- Consider opportunity types of giving (e.g. effect investing)

- Engage your own circle of relatives and community

Take Action!

- Identify a motive or charity that resonates with you

- Research and study extra approximately the organization

- Develop a giving plan (time, money, resources)

- Get concerned and have an effective effect!

By giving again and creating an effective effect, you may be accomplishing economic freedom at the same time as additionally creating a distinction within the lives of others. Congratulations, you've got reached the very last bankruptcy of "Wealth Wise"! We hope this ee-e book has stimulated and empowered you to acquire economic freedom and have a satisfying life.

CONCLUSION

Congratulations on completing "Wealth Wise"! By now, you've gotcomplete information about private finance, investing, and wealth creation. You have discovered the way to set economic desires, budget, invest, control debt, construct credit, and deliver return for your community.

Remember, accomplishing economic freedom is an adventure, now no longer a destination. It calls for discipline, patience, and persistence. But the rewards arereally well worth it-economic security, peace of thought, and the capacity to live on your very own terms.

As you keep on your economic adventure, preserve in thoughts the subsequent key takeaways:

- Financial freedom is achievable, irrespective of your earnings or background.

- Education and know-how are the keys to creating knowledgeable economic decisions.

- Discipline and consistency are vital for accomplishing economic desires.

- Giving return and creating a tremendous effect are critical components of genuine wealth.

We hope "Wealth Wise" has stimulated and empowered you to take manage of your price range and construct a brighter economic future. Remember to live knowledgeable, live disciplined, and constantly preserve your long- time period desires in thoughts.

Thank you for reading "Wealth Wise"! We want you all of the exceptional to your adventure of economic freedom!

www.ingramcontent.com/pod-product-compliance
Lightning Source LLC
Chambersburg PA
CBHW070141230526
45472CB00004B/1627